GHOST TOWNS

of the
CRIPPLE CREEK DISTRICT

By
LELAND FEITZ

Published by
LITTLE LONDON PRESS
284 Sevo Place
Colorado Springs, Colorado

Leland Feitz

The author has been a part-time resident of Cripple Creek since 1954 with a full time interest. *Ghost Towns of the Cripple Creek District* is his 5th book about the great gold camp. His Little London Press has published twenty Western Americana titles with a combined circulation of over 100,000.

Copyright 1974
Leland Feitz

The Cover

A building in Elkton is by Breta Lighty, Cripple Creek area resident, whose works have been shown in galleries in Colorado, New Mexico, Arizona, and Texas.

INTRODUCTION

by

Dayton Lummis Jr., Director
Cripple Creek District Museum

Cripple Creek and Victor sit at opposite ends of the great gold mining district, one with the name known around the world, and the other calling itself "The City of Mines." Scattered around the District, however, were smaller, less-known towns, located variously by their proximity to large mines, or by some early settler's hope that his land would develop into a flourishing town. These smaller towns all felt that they had the potential to rival Cripple Creek or Victor; they had stores, banks, service facilities, but as the District developed, rail and trolley lines made movement easier from the larger towns, both back and forth, and to the mines; commerce and recreation concentrated in Cripple Creek and Victor, as miners and business people relocated in the centers of population. The inevitable process of decay began for the smaller towns, and fate decreed something other than permanence for places like Mound City, Altman, Arequa, or Anaconda. In the declining years after 1900, the peak year of producttion in the District, only a handful of hardy souls hung on in the smaller towns, people beating against the tides of shrinking production and consolidation. The locations of these towns today are mostly grassy sites with only the faintest outlines where buildings stood, or in a few cases, a crumbling collection of lonely and deserted structures slowly succumbing to the elements — and to the depredations of people.

A tour of the sites of these satellite towns gives one some idea of the geographic and economic diversity of the District, and a feeling for the the declining days of the area. Cows graze near the ruins of once productive mills, and winds swirl around empty houses from which miners once trudged in all kinds of weather to their jobs beneath the ground. The names of these towns call to mind vanished dreams, and these lonely sites are reminders of impermanence of things in this world. Leland Feitz's book now documents the locations of these smaller towns and the roles they played in the District seventy-five years ago. In perspective we see them as places where people lived and worked, and nourished aspirations — adding vitality to the whole of the Cripple Creek Mining District.

The fifteen little cities of the Cripple Creek District are located on the above map.

ALTA VISTA

Once a stage stop, Alta Vista (Spanish for High View), three miles south of Victor, became an important railroad center when the Florence and Cripple Creek pushed up Phantom Canyon into the Cripple Creek District. From 1894, it was the narrow gauge classification yard for the entire District and was almost always jammed with trainloads of gold ore, coal, mining machinery, and supplies.

As many as six passenger trains passed through Alta Vista every day during its early years. It was one of the busiest little places in the camp.

But Alta Vista never grew into too much of a town. There were just a few dwellings for section men around the tiny wooden depot.

The Florence and Cripple Creek went out of business in 1912. Alta Vista folded.

The last landmark of Alta Vista. The tiny depot, built in 1894 has now been moved to Victor and has served as an information center.

ALTMAN

At an elevation of 10,620 feet above sea level, Altman, in a scenic saddle between Bull Hill and Bull Cliff, was one of the highest incorporated cities in the world. Platted in 1893 and named for Sam Altman, an early settler, the lofty little town was near the Pharmacist, Deadwood, Zenobia, Isabella, Buena Vista, and Victor gold mines. A strong union town, Altman was one of the headquarters of the mine workers during both the District's bloody labor wars.

By 1897 some 2,000 people lived in Altman and on the hills sloping down from it. There was a sort of a "main street" lined with a string of flimsy, false-fronted pine buildings housing three grocery stores, five saloons, two hotels, several restaurants and boarding houses. Altman had one school house and a couple of churches.

By 1900 Altman's population had slipped to well under 1,000. There was a mass evacuation during the 1904 labor war. By 1908 Altman was well on its way to being a ghost town. Now there are just a few crumbling shacks.

Altman in 1894 was just starting to take shape. The high altitude boom town was then one of the camp's fastest growing communities.

With Pikes Peak, nine miles away, as a backdrop, little Altman had one of the most magnificent settings of any city in the country. About 2,000 people lived there in 1897.

Many of Altman's unpainted shacks spilled off the top of the hill on which it was built toward the Isabella and other gold mines which supported it.

No "City Beautiful," Altman, nevertheless, tried to dress up its main drag with a row of evergreens. (Denver Public Library Western Collection)

Downtown Altman. Five saloons, three grocery stores, two hotels, and a variety of other businesses faced its board-walked main street. (Penrose Public Library)

Bull Hill Camp of Colorado State Militia during the 1894 labor war. Altman is in the background. (Cripple Creek District Museum)

Not much is left of "one of the highest incorporated cities in the world." This is Altman's main street, summer of 1974. (Photo by Dayton Lummis, Jr.)

ANACONDA

Founded in 1894, Anaconda filled the upper reaches of Squaw Gulch with a 1900 population of well over 1,000 persons. About one-third of the way between Cripple Creek and Victor, the little settlement was, for the most part, supported by the celebrated Anaconda, Mary McKinney, Morning Glory, Chicken Hawk, Dolly Varden, and Doctor Jack Pot mines.

Even though it was quite close to big Cripple Creek, Anaconda still had an active business center of its own. Two blocks of false-fronted buildings housed hotels, saloons, drug and grocery stores. There were doctors, lawyers, printers, music teachers, dressmakers, an optician and one artist. There was an especially nice white frame school house and several churches. Texas "Hello, Sucker!" Guinan of New York speakeasy fame who once lived in Squaw Gulch played an organ in one of them.

During the winter of 1904, a fire pretty well leveled Anaconda. No effort was made to rebuild it. The people just moved on to either Cripple Creek or Victor. It's been a ghost town since. All that remains are a few foundations, the walls of the jail house, and evidences of the streets.

Anaconda strung along Squaw Gulch for over half a mile. It was one of the District's greatest concentrations of population.

With Anaconda in the gulch below, a Florence and Cripple Creek passenger train is seen steaming toward Victor. Later, two other railroads and a street car line passed through the metropolis of Squaw Gulch.

Anaconda grew all the way up Squaw Gulch to the Anaconda Mine on Gold Hill. The narrow gauge tracks of the Florence and Cripple Creek Railroad are in the foreground (Denver Public Library Western Collection)

An Anaconda street. The mine is the famed Mary McKinney.

No conformity here; each Anaconda home had its own personality. (Denver Public Library Western Collection)

The Deerhorn, one of Squaw Gulch's posh inns. (Denver Public Library Western Collection)

Anaconda's little white frame school house was the pride of the community. (Denver Public Library Western Collection)

The celebrated Mary McKinney Mine provided jobs for many men of Anaconda. A few buildings of "downtown Anaconda" are in the foreground. (Penrose Public Library)

The walls of Anaconda's old jail house frame the few buildings remaining at the Anaconda Mine. (Photo by Dayton Lummis, Jr.)

AREQUA

Platted sometime before 1890, Arequa was the oldest town site in the Cripple Creek District. But even though it had a head start, it never amounted to much more than a scattering of cabins with a population of a hundred or so. "Arequa while it has had no boom, neither has it had a set back," wrote a reporter up from Colorado Springs to tour the town in 1893.

Ben Requa, an early settler, founded the place between Beacon Hill and Squaw Mountain and had great plans for it. The principal streets were named for presidents of the United States. The town itself, like the gulch in which it stood, was to have been named for the founding father, but somehow the "A" got tossed in and what should have been Requa became Arequa.

Requa's choice for a town site wasn't very good. He platted it on the steep slopes of Arequa Gulch where building was difficult. Then, too, most of the big strikes were made some distance from it. Arequa didn't last long.

Most of old Arequa is now buried under a Golden Cycle Mill tailings pond.

Timber from the District's once-wooded hills was used to build the early towns. Arequa, in this 1892 photograph, is starting to take shape. (Denver Public Library Western Collection)

A few buildings of Arequa can be seen at the foot of Beacon Hill. The Prince Albert, Gold Dollar and Beacon Mines were located here.

The Arequa Mill, 1903. (Cripple Creek District Museum)

Much of old Arequa is buried under the tailings pond of the Golden Cycle Mill. The big mine on Beacon Hill is the Gold Dollar.

BARRY

Barry mushroomed up in Squaw Gulch just east of Mound City. The little shanty-type town was founded in 1891 by Horace Barry one of the District's earliest prospectors. Barry claimed his town was the "cultural center of the gold camp!"

A peak population of a few hundred was reached in 1893 when the mills of Squaw Gulch were all going full blast. Then, Barry had a post office and a small business district centering around The Squaw Gulch Amusement Club.

Barry slipped from the scene by the turn of the century after the local mills closed. The people who had worked there moved on to other jobs in other parts of the camp.

Nothing at all remains of Barry.

Barry, between Mound City and Anaconda, was a slab and canvas sort of place. The Blue Bell Mine, right above Barry, was one of the District's leading early producers. (Denver Public Library Western Collection)

Barry, November, 1891. Then, it was one of the District's boom towns.

BULL HILL

The major Cripple Creek yards of the Midland Terminal Railroad were at Bull Hill. And while the yards were extensive and there was a tremendous amount of activity there, between 1894 and 1949, Bull Hill never amounted to very much as a town. Just a few bunk houses and sheds clustered around the yards and the little red depot.

Bull Hill, at the top of Victor Pass with an elevation of 10,199 feet, was the highest point on the Midland Terminal line. It was located between Cameron and Goldfield.

There is much evidence today of the great railroading activity that took place there. The depot itself was moved to Cripple Creek in the 1960's and serves as the ticket office and gift shop for the popular Cripple Creek and Victor Narrow Gauge Railroad.

Bull Hill station, at 10,199 feet elevation, was the highest point reached by the Midland Terminal Railroad on its climb from Colorado Springs to Cripple Creek.

Bull Hill station on its way to Cripple Creek. The old building, completely restored, is now the ticket office for the Cripple Creek and Victor Narrow Gauge Railroad.

CAMERON

First called Gassey, then Grassey, little Cameron was never home to but a few hundred people. But it was often the playground of thousands! For Cameron was the home of Pinnacle Park.

While no Coney Island, Pinnacle Park, nevertheless, had dance pavilions, a ball park with bleachers seating 1,000, picnic areas, a variety of restaurants, a few rides, and a mini-zoo. The people of the District loved it! Over 9,000 of them turned up at Pinnacle Park on Labor Day in 1900. The gate admission was 10c.

Founded early in 1900 by the Woods brothers, who also fathered Victor, Cameron was beautifully situated on a grassy meadow at the foot of a hill covered with tall pine trees. Both the Midland Terminal and the Colorado Springs and Cripple Creek District Railroad passed through Cameron. A tiny brick business district faced wide Cameron Avenue. A newspaper called *The Golden Cresent* was published for a short time.

After the popularity of the park faded, Cameron's population slumped and by 1910 it was pretty much a ghost town. A few scattered foundations and the zoo's bear pits are about all that can be seen today.

The Midland Terminal depot at Cameron. Until the line was completed into Cripple Creek, stages from that city met the trains here.

A dance pavilion at Pinnacle Park, the District's playground. (Cripple Creek District Museum)

There was a variety of restaurants at Pinnacle Park. This was one of them. (Cripple Creek District Museum)

The railroad tracks at Pinnacle Park were crossed by a rustic bridge which matched the buildings themselves. Frequently scheduled trains and weekend and holiday "specials" brought people to the park.

The Pinnacle Park Zoo. The animals have been gone for well over half a century, but remnants of the cages can still be seen. The Park covered thirty acres and represented a $32,000 investment.

ELKTON

Not a planned or an incorporated city, Elkton just started growing up in 1893 around Sam and George Bernard's huge mine of the same name. They called their discovery the Elkton after finding a pair of elk horns at the site. Including those who lived down in Arequa Gulch and over on Beacon Hill, Elkton's 1900 population was about 2,500.

At about the halfway point between Cripple Creek and Victor, Elkton had a fairly good little business district including five hotels, three grocery stores, two drug stores, a book store, a cigar store, two doctors, one dressmaker, a couple barber shops and enough saloons. Trains steamed though Elkton twenty-four hours a day. It was on all three railroad lines and the Low Line streetcar route.

Like other little towns in the District, Elkton never fully recovered from the labor wars. Even so, the Elkton Mine continued to be a heavy producer until about 1916, keeping the town alive. Some of Elkton's old houses and business buildings still stand.

Elkton grew in a helter-skelter fashion in Arequa Gulch above and below the rich Elkton Gold Mine. (Denver Public Library Western Collection)

Sam and George Bernard's Elkton Mine produced gold worth well over $16,000,000. It created the town's greatest payroll.

Little remains of Elkton's once busy commercial center. (Photo by Dayton Lummis, Jr.)

GOLDFIELD

Many of the lesser settlements of the Cripple Creek District were never more than mining camps. But, Goldfield *was* a city! And while it has not been a city for over half a century now, neither is it a ghost town. True, it is a ghost of what it was, but there are still a few people living in it. Fact is, there has been a little growth during the last couple of years. The permanent population is back up to about 35!

The most favorably situated city in the District, Goldfield was platted on a fairly level spot at the foot of Battle Mountain and Bull Hill near all the big gold mines. Founded in 1895 by the owners of the giant Portland Mine, it was not incorporated as a city until 1899. By then it was the third biggest city in the gold camp. Some 3,500 people lived there.

Even though the city of Victor was only about a mile and a half away, Goldfield still had an active little business district where Ninth Street intersected Main and Independence. The 1900 Cripple Creek District Directory indicates that Goldfield had five grocery stores, two drug stores, five hotels, half a dozen saloons, four churches, three schools, four doctors, two dentists, and one tamale peddler. There was a daily newspaper called *The Goldfield Leader* and a weekly called *The Goldfield Times.*

Both the Golden Circle Railroad, a narrow gauge related to the Florence & Cripple Creek, and the Colorado Springs and Cripple Creek District Railroad passed through town. The Midland Terminal Station was within easy walking distance.

When Teller County was formed in 1899, Goldfield vied for the title of county seat. Losing out to larger Cripple Creek, Goldfield continued to improve itself and became the most attractive family town in the District.

Goldfield, at the foot of Big Bull Mountain, as seen from Battle Mountain. Unlike some of the District's other satellite communities, Goldfield was a real city. (State Historical Society of Colorado)

Goldfield's bustling business district. The big building in the background housed the La Bella Electric Co.

Goldfield and Independence, just above it, had a combined population of some 5,000 persons. This was the very hub of the gold camp. (Penrose Public Library)

Goldfield was a city of modest, but neat, little homes. The Independence and Portland Mines can be seen on Battle Mountain in the background. They provided jobs for many of the men living in Goldfield.

The Goldfield School. There was a second school in Goldfield; seventeen others in the Cripple Creek District. (State Historical Society of Colorado)

The Goldfield City Hall. Alone now, it was once surrounded by miner's cottages with well kept gardens.

GILLETT

A flourishing little city between 1894 and 1905, Gillett's population once reached over 1,200. Supported by the Midland Terminal Railroad, smelters, reduction mills and a few unimportant mines, Gillett, named for an official of the Midland Terminal, was five miles from Cripple Creek and the northern gateway to the District. First called Cripple City, Gillett was also the "Las Vegas" of the camp, with a racetrack and gambling casino.

Gillett was the only city in the District to be built on level ground. It had the only bank in the District except those in Cripple Creek and Victor. *The Gillett Forum* was the only regular newspaper published in the camp except for those in the two major cities and Goldfield. It was one of a few Colorado cities to own its very own water and light company. And, it had the West's only bull ring!

An early writer called Gillett very raw and very western. Another called it the District's bachelor town since so few families lived there.

By 1920, the population had dwindled to about 50. Soon they all left and Gillett, for the most part, was simply plowed up and returned to ranch land. Today, only the walls of the Catholic Church, one house, a few foundations, and traces of the streets and race track can be seen.

Early Gillett. It was a railroad town. Shops and round-houses for the Midland Terminal Railroad were located there.

The Midland Terminal Depot at Gillett. Eight passenger trains once passed through it every day on their way to and from the Cripple Creek District.

Most of Gillett's false-fronted business buildings faced Parker Street. Later, in an effort to dress it up, little aspen trees were planted down its sides.

The Woodruff Store, one of Gillett's supermarkets. (Denver Public Library Western Collection)

The Gillett Bull Ring, built in 1895 in Sportsman's Park, seated 5,000. The insert shows a copy of the ticket printed for The Mexican Fiesta and Bull Fight, Gillett's biggest blowout.

Gillett's popular Monte Carlo Lake and Casino. (Denver Public Library Western Collection)

The Monte Carlo Casino later became Gillett School (Denver Public Library Western Collection)

As late as 1940, Gillett's little Catholic church still stood. (Denver Public Library Western Collection, photo by M. S. Wolle)

There are still some evidences that Gillett was once a city. (Denver Public Library Western Collection, photo by M. S. Wolle)

INDEPENDENCE

Independence, originally called Macon and Hull City, was the District's most typical mining town. Not much planning went into Independence. It just grew up around the Hull City, Vindicator, and Findley mines, and spilled off down Montgomery Gulch toward Goldfield. A town of rough lumber shacks dotted here and there between the mines, it looked exactly like a mining town should.

Officially platted in 1894 and named for the Independence Mine a few miles away, the town never quite lived up to the expectations of its founding fathers. They advertised: "The youngest and the most promising town in the great gold camp. In twelve months it will be the commercial center of the great Cripple Creek District."

Even so, the 1900 population reached over 1,500. It was served by two railroads and one of the District's two streetcar lines. The Silver Bell, Golden Circle, and Cole Brothers Music Hall were among the liveliest saloons in the state.

Several people still lived in Independence as late as the mid-1950's. Now, it is completely deserted but quite a few of the old mine buildings and miners homes remain.

Early Independence was a cluster of log cabins and pine shacks on an almost untouched Bull Hill.

Independence sprawled all over the face of Bull Hill during the mid-1890's. Then, some 1,500 people lived there. (Denver Public Library Western Collection)

Much of early Independence just sprung up without planning around the Hull City Mine. Beyond it is the Vindicator. The big white building was Independence School. (State Historical Society of Colorado)

Independence today. No one has lived there since the mid-1950's.

Once again a cow pasture. That is what it was before gold was discovered and it became one of the camp's boom towns. Independence has gone the full circle.

LAWRENCE

Until Victor was established, Lawrence was the commercial center for the southern part of the camp. One of the District's first towns, Lawrence was founded in 1892 along Wilson Creek just down the hill from where Victor was to be built. A town of log cabins, Lawrence was once home to some 300 people. It took its name from an area ranch.

The community was supported by a large gold extraction mill, a brick yard, and a slaughterhouse. The last industry continued until late in the camp's life. But most of the people moved up the hill to Victor after it started to boom as the District's second largest city.

Lawrence's major contribution to the area came through important experiments conducted there with the chlorination process in ore refining.

Only a few buildings and traces of Lawrence's streets can be found today.

Lawrence, on Wilson Creek, was the earliest settlement in the southern part of the camp. This is how it looked in 1892. That's Squaw Mountain in the background.

The Lawrence Gold Extracting Company's mill. On Wilson Creek in Lawrence, it was one of the first mills in the southern part of the mining district. (Penrose Public Library)

Lawrence, summer of '74. The view is toward Wilson Creek and Straub Mountain. (Photo by Dayton Lummis, Jr.)

MIDWAY

While not exactly a town, Midway, halfway between Cripple Creek and Victor, has, nevertheless, been a well known site since the days streetcars passed through it. At an elevation of 10,487 feet, it was the highest point in the gold camp to have streetcar service.

There was a sprinkling of miners shacks at Midway and around the nearby Vista Grande Loop of the Golden Circle Railroad. Probably no more than fifty people lived there. But at the turn of the century, many hundreds of miners passed through Midway every day on their way to work at the Wild Horse and other Bull Hill mines.

Few men passed through Midway without stopping at the popular Grand View Saloon. It served as a "watering hole" and waiting room for the miners who traveled to and from their work on the High Line streetcar line.

Even though it is in a sad state of repair, the old Grand View Saloon building still stands and, the view from it is grand indeed.

Midway at the foot of Bull Hill. The mine above the little settlement is the Wild Horse.

Midway's Grand View was one of the gold camp's most popular saloons. It was full of miners, day and night, who stopped there between shifts at the big mines on Bull Hill.

A unique camp, miners rode thoroughly modern streetcars from their homes to their work. This High Line car is approaching Midway.

MOUND CITY

Originally called Squaw Village, Mound City sprawled over the area where Squaw Gulch met Cripple Creek, just south of Cripple Creek town. Settled in 1891, but never incorporated, Mound City grew up around a cluster of mills which supported it.

Between 500 and 600 people lived there by 1893 in a random scattering of log cabins and board shacks. There was a general store, four hotels, and a one-room school house. It was, according to an 1892 writer: "As prettily situated and lively a little camp as there is in the state."

As its pioneer mills were replaced with more modern ones closer to the mines, Mound City's population drifted on up the gulch to Anaconda and other cities in the District. By the turn of the century, Mound City was almost totally deserted.

Now a little remains of the mills, and a few traces of the once busy streets can be seen.

Mound City, in 1893, was one of the liveliest camps in the Cripple Creek District. Most of the men who lived there worked in the huge Brodie Mill. (State Historical Society of Colorado)

One of the District's early mills, the Brodie, at Mound City. (Cripple Creek District Museum)

Mound City's Rosebud Mill stood for only two years. It burned to the ground in July of 1894. (Cripple Creek District Museum)

The sign stands where two of Mound City's busy streets once intersected. (Photo by Dayton Lummis Jr.)

The ruins of the Brodie Mill as they look today. (Photo by Dayton Lummis Jr.)

WINFIELD

The Cripple Creek mining district had just one company-like town. It was Winfield, sometimes called Summit, sometimes Stratton. Some five miles east of Cripple Creek on Globe Hill, Winfield was a good looking town of big, impressive red brick and white frame buildings in a pine forest. The buildings housed offices, dormitories, and dining halls. There was no business district. People who lived there hopped on High Line street cars and did their shopping and playing in Cripple Creek or Victor.

Winfield was built in 1900 by Winfield Scott Stratton of the famed Independence Mine. From there, Stratton hoped to conduct an operation which was to lead to the core of "bowl of gold" from which he believed all of Cripple Creek's wealth spewed. Stratton, the District's first millionaire died before the theory was ever proved.

Winfield's buildings were demolished before much of the townsite was buried under tons of ore hauled there to be processed through heap leaching.

Winfield Scott Stratton, the District's first millionaire and greatest philanthropist

Winfield's big red brick buildings housed offices and laboratories.

Not exactly a family town, most of the men who worked in Winfield lived in boarding houses.

AND THEN THERE WERE MORE

Smaller and lesser known settlements within the Cripple Creek Mining District included DUTCHTOWN, some two miles south of Victor and HOLLYWOOD, a sub-division joining Victor on the East. MARIGOLD, a station on the Canon City stage road was a few miles south of Cripple Creek. LOVE, in west Beaver Creek Valley, about three miles east of the District was another stage stop. It was on an early wagon road between the mining camp and Colorado Springs.

While they could not be thought of as towns, there were a few occupied shacks surrounding such places as DYER and LOS ANGELES and PORTLAND, LILLIE, VINDICATOR and EAGLE JUNCTIONS. These were all railroad junctions, sidings or locations between Battle Mountain and Bull Hill. Just above Cripple Creek on Gold Hill, where the tracks of the Colorado Springs & Cripple Creek District Railroad crossed the tracks of the High Line Electric, there was a place called FAIRVIEW, later renamed BADGER.

There were also a few nearby settlements on the three railroad approaches to the District. CLYDE, on the Colorado Springs & Cripple Creek District Railroad was a lumber camp with considerable railroad facilities. Scenic Cathedral Park, with shelters and a baseball diamond, was just west of the little town. A favorite picnic spot of Cripple Creek District people, special excursion trains were often run there from the mining camp. MIDLAND, on the Midland-Terminal Railroad between Divide and Gillett, consisted of a wooden water tank and a few section houses strung out along a fairly long rail siding. WILBUR, on the Florence and Cripple Creek Railroad south of Victor in Phantom Canyon, had a 1900 population of about sixty people, a post office, school house, and a few railroad facilities.

Other Little London Press booklets about the Cripple Creek District:

CRIPPLE CREEK, THE WORLD'S GREATEST GOLD CAMP

CRIPPLE CREEK RAILROADS

MYERS AVENUE, CRIPPLE CREEK'S REDLIGHT DISTRICT

VICTOR, COLORADO'S "CITY OF MINES"

SEEING CRIPPLE CREEK, A SELF CONDUCTED TOUR